OHIO COUNTY PUBLIC LIBRARY
WHEELING, W

W9-DBH-272

OHIO COUNTY PUBLIC LIBRARY
WHEELING, WV 26003

Months of the Year

January

by Robyn Brode

Reading consultant: Susan Nations, M.Ed.,
author/literacy coach/consultant

JUV
E
B784j
2003

JUL 2 5 2003

1270161965

Please visit our web site at: www.earlyliteracy.cc
For a free color catalog describing Weekly Reader® Early Learning Library's list
of high-quality books, call 1-877-445-5824 (USA) or 1-800-387-3178 (Canada).
Weekly Reader® Early Learning Library's fax: (414) 336-0164.

Library of Congress Cataloging-in-Publication Data

Brode, Robyn.
    January / by Robyn Brode.
      p. cm. — (Months of the year)
    Summary: An introduction to some of the characteristics, events, and activities
of the month of January.
    ISBN 0-8368-3576-X (lib. bdg.)
    ISBN 0-8368-3612-X (softcover)
    1. January—Juvenile literature. 2. Holidays—United States—Juvenile literature.
[1. January.] I. Title.
GT4803.B766   2003
394.261—dc21   2002034302

First published in 2003 by
Weekly Reader® Early Learning Library
330 West Olive Street, Suite 100
Milwaukee, WI 53212 USA

Copyright © 2003 by Weekly Reader® Early Learning Library

Editor: Robyn Brode
Art direction, design, and page production: Leonardo Montenegro with Orange Avenue
Models: Olivia Byers-Strans, Isabella Leary, Madeline Leary
Weekly Reader® Early Learning Library art direction: Tammy Gruenewald
Weekly Reader® Early Learning Library editor: Mark J. Sachner

Photo credits: Cover, pp. 13, 19 © Comstock Images; title, pp. 7, 9, 11 (both), 21
© Getty Images; p. 15 © PictureQuest; p. 17 © Hulton Archive/Getty Images

All rights reserved. No part of this book may be reproduced, stored in a retrieval system,
or transmitted in any form or by any means, electronic, mechanical, photocopying,
recording, or otherwise, without the prior written permission of the copyright holder.

Printed in the United States of America

1 2 3 4 5 6 7 8 9 07 06 05 04 03

Note to Educators and Parents

Reading is such an exciting adventure for young children! They are beginning to integrate their oral language skills with written language. To help this process along, books must be meaningful, colorful, engaging, and interesting; they should invite young readers to make inquiries about the world around them.

Months of the Year is a new series of books designed to help children learn more about each of the twelve months. In each book, young readers will learn about festivals, celebrations, weather, and other interesting facts about each month.

Each book is specially designed to support the young reader in the reading process. The familiar topics are appealing to young children and invite them to re-read — again and again. The full-color photographs and enhanced text further support the student during the reading process.

These books are designed to be read within an instructional guided reading group. This small group setting allows beginning readers to work with a fluent adult model as they make meaning from the text. After children develop fluency with the text and content, the book can be read independently. Children and adults alike will find these books supportive, engaging, and fun!

— *Susan Nations, M.Ed., author, literacy coach, and consultant in literacy development*

January is the first month of the year. January has 31 days.

January

1	2	3	4	5	6	7
8	9	10	11	12	13	14
15	16	17	18	19	20	21
22	23	24	25	26	27	28
29	30	31				

January 1 is called New Year's Day. It is a holiday for people all over the world because it is the first day of every new year.

Sometimes Chinese New Year begins in January. Sometimes it begins in February. There is always a big parade.

January is a winter month. Some places are cold and snowy in winter. Some places are not.

In places where
it snows, kids like
to make snowpeople.

Have you ever made
a snowperson?

For most students, winter vacation ends in January. Then it is time to go back to school.

In January we celebrate the birthday of Dr. Martin Luther King, Jr. He was a leader who wanted all people to be treated the same.

Dr. Martin Luther King, Jr.

In class, students learn about Dr. King and think about his words of hope for the future.

When January ends,
it is time for February
to begin.

Glossary

New Year's Day — a holiday that falls on the first day of a calendar year

parade — a public celebration when musical bands and people in costumes walk down the street

snowperson — big balls of snow put on top of each other to look like a person

Months of the Year

1	January	7	July
2	February	8	August
3	March	9	September
4	April	10	October
5	May	11	November
6	June	12	December

Seasons of the Year

Winter	Summer
Spring	Fall

About the Author

Robyn Brode wrote the *Going Places* children's book series and was the editor for *Get Out!*, which won the 2002 Disney Award for Hands-On Activities. She has been an editor, writer, and teacher in the book publishing field for many years. She earned a Bachelors in English Literature from the University of California at Berkeley.